ANIMALS IN MOTION

HOW ANIMALS SWIM, JUMP, SLITHER AND GLIDE

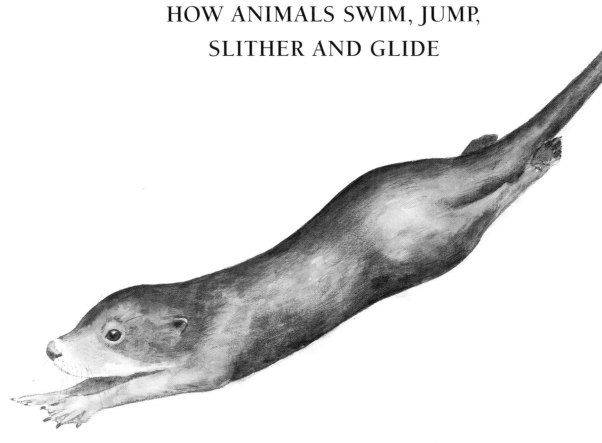

WRITTEN BY PAMELA HICKMAN

ILLUSTRATED BY PAT STEPHENS

Kids Can Press

My thanks to Pat Stephens for her beautiful and detailed illustrations,
to Marie Bartholomew for the book design and to my editors Laura Ellis and Laurie Wark.

For Angela

Kids Can Press acknowledges the support of the Ontario Arts
Council, the Canada Council for the Arts and the Government of
Canada, through the BPIDP, for our publishing activity. Canadä

Published in Canada by
Kids Can Press Ltd.
29 Birch Avenue
Toronto, ON M4V 1E2

Published in the U.S. by
Kids Can Press Ltd.
4500 Witmer Industrial Estates
Niagara Falls, NY 14305-1386

Edited by Laura Ellis and Laurie Wark
Designed by Marie Bartholomew
Printed in Hong Kong by Wing King Tong Co. Ltd.

CM 00 0 9 8 7 6 5 4 3 2 1
CM PA 00 0 9 8 7 6 5 4 3 2 1

Canadian Cataloguing in Publication Data

Hickman, Pamela

 Animals in motion: how animals swim, jump, slither
and glide

ISBN 1-55074-573-5 (bound)
ISBN 1-55074-575-1 (pbk.)

1. Animal locomotion - Juvenile literature. I. Stephens,
Pat. II. Title.

QP301.H52 2000   j573.7'9   C99-932111-0

Kids Can Press is a Nelvana company

Contents

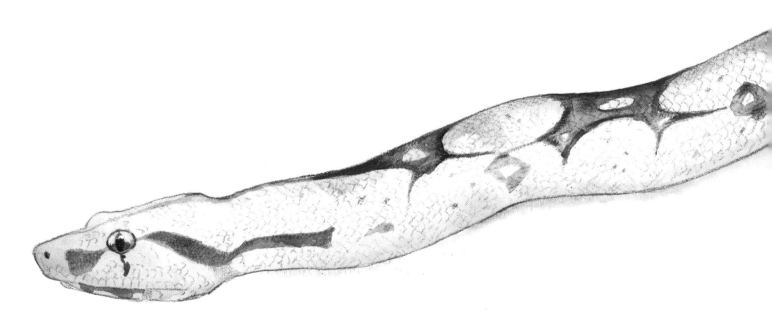

Introduction

Imagine outrunning a car on the highway, the way a cheetah can. Or jumping a high fence in a single bound, like a kangaroo. What if you could glide over the ocean for hours like an albatross, or fly backward the way a hummingbird does? Animals come in all shapes and sizes, and their bodies are adapted, or specially suited, to move in certain ways. Whether sliding over a slimy trail like a snail, or darting through the water like a fish, animals move about to find food or a mate, seek shelter and escape danger.

People sometimes put on special equipment to help them move around better. In these pages you'll discover animals with their own built-in flippers, diving goggles, snowshoes and cleats. There are activities and experiments to help you compare your speed and jumping ability to that of other animals. Discover some fancy animal feet and then check to see if any of them have visited your neighborhood recently. You'll get a close-up look at some unusual animals, meet a fish that flies and a frog that climbs trees, and much more!

Basilisk Lizard

Swimmers and floaters

If you want to swim faster, you can put on a pair of flippers. To breathe underwater, people use snorkels or scuba tanks. And to keep warm in cold water, divers wear special diving suits. Animals that live in the water have many adaptations, or special features, that help them move around in their habitat. Being a good swimmer or diver helps an animal catch its food more easily, avoid predators, attract a mate and possibly travel to a new home if its habitat is destroyed. Beavers are well known for their dam-building skills, but they're also excellent swimmers and divers.

6

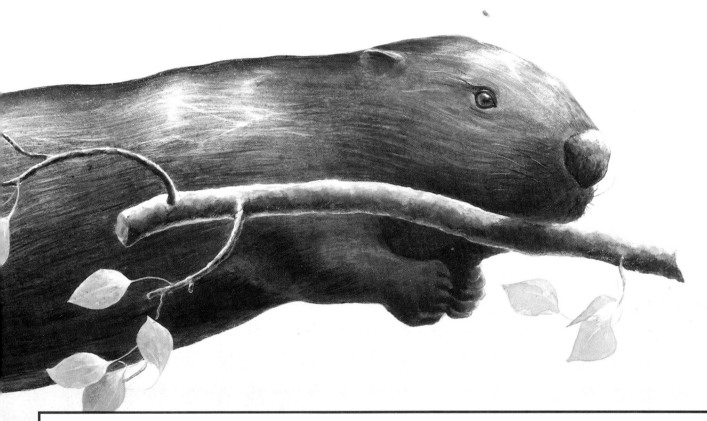

If you were a beaver ...

- you would have webbed hind feet to help you swim.
- your broad, flat tail would help you steer through the water.
- you could close tiny flaps in your nose and ears when you dive so that water couldn't get in.
- you would have a set of see-through eyelids, like goggles, that close over your eyes to protect them while you are underwater.
- you would spread special oil from your body over your fur to make it waterproof.

Go fish

Try pushing the palm of your hand through a basin of water. Now turn your hand sideways and move it through the water again. You should find that your hand glides through the water much more easily when it is turned to the side. When something moves through the water, it has to push the water out of its way. Since the side of your hand is narrower than the palm, it has to push less water aside and it can move with less effort. A typical fish's body has a narrow head and tail, and a slightly thicker middle. As a fish swims, its head moves from side to side, pushing the water out of its way. As the water moves back, it closes in behind the fish, helping to push the fish forward.

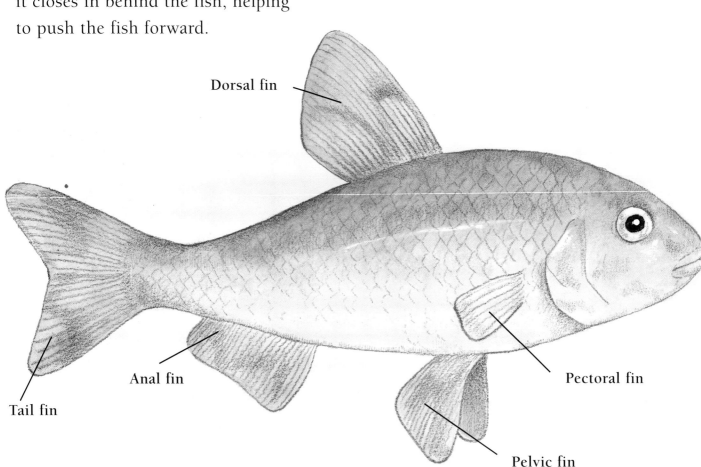

Dorsal fin

Pectoral fin

Anal fin

Tail fin

Pelvic fin

A fish's fins also help it move through the water. Each fin is connected to muscles. The dorsal and pelvic fins work to keep the fish upright. Pectoral fins help the fish turn in the water and keep its balance. The tail fin is used for steering and for powering the fish through the water.

Jellyfish

A jellyfish isn't a fish at all. It is closely related to sea anemones and corals. Its jelly-like body sac is shaped like an umbrella that floats through the water, carried by currents and the wind. Jellyfish also move slowly up and down in the water by relaxing and contracting their muscles. They can move quickly to escape underwater danger, too. Here's how they do it.

1. The jellyfish tightens the circle of muscles around its outer rim so that it looks like an umbrella closing.

Jellyfish

2. When the jellyfish relaxes the muscles, water is sucked through the animal's mouth and fills its stomach.

3. Next, the jellyfish quickly tenses its muscles again, forcing the water out of its stomach so fast that the escaping water rockets the animal upward.

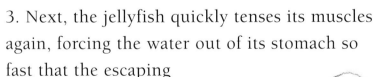

What a blast!

Use a turkey baster or large eyedropper to imitate the way a jellyfish's body works while it is swimming.

Put the open end of the tube in a bowl of water and hold the rubber bulb end of the baster or eyedropper. Squeeze the rubber bulb hard, like the jellyfish tightening its muscles. Now relax your hand. You should notice that water rushes into the tube. That's because you have squeezed all of the air out of the tube, creating a vacuum. When you let go, water rushes in to fill the empty space.

Squeeze the rubber bulb again and watch as the water blasts out of the tube. This jet of water would shoot the jellyfish upward.

Wings underwater

Not all fish have the same shape. Skates and rays live on the bottom of the ocean, and their special pancake shape moves easily through the water as they hunt for food. Their large, wing-like pectoral fins surround their bodies from head to tail and move in a rippling motion, as if the fish were flying underwater. Skates and rays use their whip-like tails for steering and for defense.

Manta Ray

You may know that penguins can't fly, but did you know that they still use their wings to get around? A penguin's narrow, pointy wings make terrific underwater flippers to help the bird swim and dive. Puffins use their short wings for flying in the air and swimming underwater.

Penguin

Puffin

Wet feet

What does a scuba diver have in common with a Duck-billed Platypus? The answer is webbed feet. People wear flippers to get more power and speed in the water. Many animals that live in the water have built-in flippers. Birds such as penguins, puffins, ducks and geese all use their broad feet to help them travel through the water. Frogs are well known for their large webbed feet, and several aquatic mammals, such as otters and beavers, also have webbed feet for swimming.

Duck-billed Platypus

Long-distance swimmers

A few people have swum across the Great Lakes and the English Channel, but some fish swim all the way across the Atlantic Ocean. Freshwater eels of North America and Europe migrate to the Sargasso Sea to lay their eggs when they are between five and eight years old. The young that hatch from the eggs swim back to either North America or Europe, where they will live and grow until their own time comes to migrate.

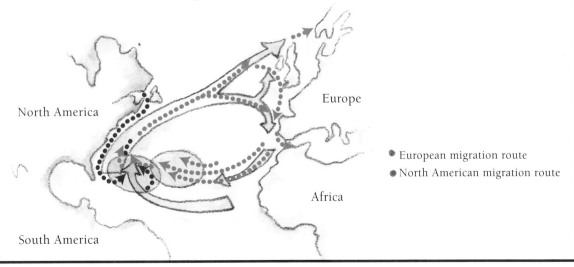

North America

Europe

Africa

South America

• European migration route
• North American migration route

Fliers and gliders

Imagine hovering over a flower, soaring as high as the clouds or gliding silently from tree to tree in the dark. Many animals can move through the air, but it takes wings to really fly. Take a look at the feathered, scaly and skin-covered wings of the creatures on these pages and find out how flying lizards and flying squirrels glide long distances without wings.

Being able to fly also allows some creatures to migrate long distances. This Rufous Hummingbird travels more than 8000 km (5000 mi.) on its round-trip flight between Alaska and Central America every year.

If you were a hummingbird ...

- you could fly forward, backward, up, down, sideways and upside down.
- you would have huge chest muscles to power your wings.
- you could hover in one place by flapping your wings.
- your wings would flap so quickly that they would make a humming sound.

Winging it

When a bird flies, it does more than just move its wings up and down. The power in a bird's flight comes when its wings move down and forward at the same time. On the downstroke, the wing's feathers are flattened out to make it more solid. The larger the wing, the more air it pushes against and the more power the bird has. When the wing comes back up, the feathers twist and separate so that the air flows right through them, and the wing moves easily back to its upright position.

Bats don't have feathers. Their wings are made of a thin layer of skin that is stretched over long finger bones. Although bat wings look very different from a bird's, bats and birds fly in a similar way.

Unlike birds and bats, insects don't have bones in their wings for support. Their wings are supported by thick veins, instead. Insects such as dragonflies have four wings. While the front wings move up, the back wings move down. Bees, moths and butterflies also have four wings, but their front and back wings move up and down at the same time. Flies have only two wings. Instead of hind wings, flies have small growths, called halteres, that help them balance.

Bat

Dragonfly

In a flap

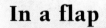

How many times can you flap your arms up and down in one second? If you were a honeybee, the answer would be 250. A hummingbird can manage 75 flaps in a second. All that flapping takes a lot of energy, so honeybees and hummingbirds spend most of their time feeding.

To save energy, the albatross uses the wind to help it glide over the ocean for hours without flapping its wings. An albatross' long, narrow wings can measure up to 3.3 m (11 ft.) from the tip of one wing to the other. That's as long as a small car!

Albatross

Graceful gliders

People use parachutes to fall more slowly through the air. Many animals, such as flying squirrels, lemurs, lizards and frogs, have built-in parachutes. When a flying squirrel wants to move from tree to tree, it jumps into the air and spreads its legs out wide. Between its front and hind legs are flaps of skin that act like mini-parachutes to slow the squirrel's fall. The squirrel steers with its tail and arrives at a lower landing place up to 45 m (150 ft.) away. Flying lizards also have large flaps of skin along their bodies to help them glide through the air. Some flying tree frogs in Asia spread out the webbing between their extra-long toes to slow down during a jump.

Flying fish

If you've ever been out on the ocean you may have seen something that looks part bird and part fish. Flying fish use their powerful tails like an outboard motor to jump into the air just above the water. Once up, they stretch out their long, wing-like pectoral fins to help them glide through the air. Some flying fish also have a pair of large pelvic fins that act like a second set of wings. If they are helped by a wind, these fish can glide up to 3 m (10 ft.) high above the water. Gliding through the air helps flying fish escape danger in the water below.

Flying fish

Flying squirrel

Make a Sugar Glider

Australia's Sugar Glider, similar to a flying squirrel, has huge flaps of skin between its legs to help it glide through the air. You can make a simple model of one using Popsicle sticks and a plastic bag.

You'll need:

3 Popsicle sticks

2 pieces of thin twine, each about 20 cm (8 in.) long

a penny or similarly sized weight

a plastic grocery bag

tape

1. Tie the three Popsicle sticks together, as shown. Tape a penny or similar weight to the bottom middle of the Popsicle sticks to help keep the sugar glider right-side-up.

2. Carefully stand on a chair and drop the sugar glider. Note how long it takes to hit the ground.

3. Cut a piece of plastic from the grocery bag, about 15 cm x 15 cm (6 in. x 6 in.).

4. Lay the stick frame on the plastic, penny side up. Tape the edge of the plastic to the end of each stick, as shown. Do not tightly stretch the plastic; it should be slack in the spaces between the sticks.

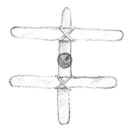

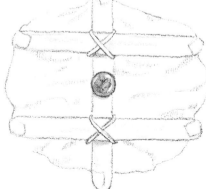

5. Hold the sugar glider so that the penny is on the bottom. Carefully stand on the chair and drop the sugar glider. Note how long it takes to reach the ground.

You should find that the sugar glider drops more slowly when the plastic is attached. The plastic acts like the animal's flaps of skin, and catches the air to slow the glider's fall.

Runners and walkers

The size and shape of an animal's feet help it move around safely in its habitat. When you walk, the bottom of your entire foot touches the ground, but if you were a bird, a cat or a dog, you would walk on your toes only. Horses, antelopes and other animals with hooves get around on just their toenails. In general, the greater the foot area that touches the ground, the slower the animal. A polar bear's large, flat feet are good for gripping

slippery ground, but they make it slow. A horse moves very fast over even ground, but easily falls on ice. Since the cheetah hunts over wide-open spaces, it must reach great speeds very quickly to attack before its prey has time to run off.

If you were a cheetah ...

- you could run faster than any creature on Earth and could reach speeds up to 112 km/h (70 m.p.h.) over a short distance. That's more than three times faster than the human record for the 100 m dash.
- you would have extra-long legs and powerful muscles in your hind legs.
- you would run by making a series of leaps.
- your long claws would help you grip the ground, like cleats on shoes.

Fancy feet

Walking across a sandy beach in summer or through deep snow in winter takes a lot of energy because you sink down as you walk. Some animals have special feet that keep them from sinking and make it easier to get around. Broad feet spread an animal's weight out over a larger area and help the animal stay on top of the snow or sand, like snowshoes. Check out the fancy feet below.

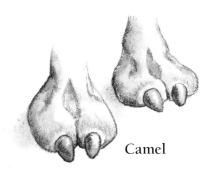

Camel

Desert camels have wide, flat pads on the bottoms of their feet to help them walk across sand without sinking. Thick soles protect their feet from hot sand.

The Fringe-toed Lizard runs on top of loose sand in the Sahara desert with help from the rows of spiny scales that edge its long hind toes.

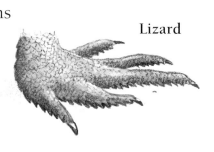

Lizard

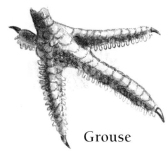

Grouse

Ruffed Grouse grow a special set of scales along their toes in winter to act like snowshoes and keep them from sinking in the snow.

Follow the feet

Whether you live in the city or the country, you can find animal tracks in your yard or neighborhood by checking out muddy trails and shorelines or fresh snow in winter. Learn to identify some of the more common tracks and try following them to see where they lead. Can you tell if the animals were walking or running by how far apart their tracks are? Here are a few footprints to help you get started.

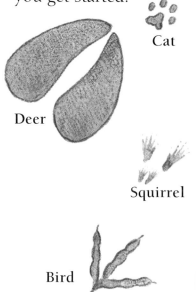

Cat

Deer

Squirrel

Bird

Big foot

Find out what it would be like to have longer and wider feet with this simple activity.

You'll need:

a sandbox raked smooth

a tape measure or ruler

a piece of heavy cardboard or thin wood, about 61 cm x 61 cm (24 in. x 24 in.)

2. Climb out of the sandbox and measure how far your feet sank into the sand.

4. Step out of the sandbox and measure how far the cardboard sank into the sand.

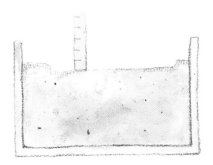

1. Step into the sandbox so that you leave your footprints in the smooth sand.

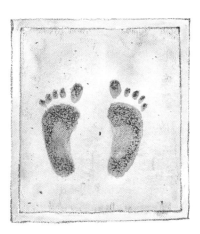

3. Smooth out the sand again. Gently lay the cardboard or wood on the sand and step onto it.

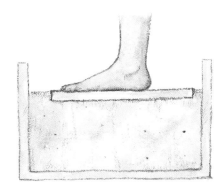

You should find that you didn't sink as far into the sand when you stood on the cardboard or wood. That's because the cardboard spread your weight out over a greater area, like larger feet would.

Walking on water

If you look sideways at a glass of water, you'll see a thick layer where the water meets the air. This layer is made of water molecules stuck tightly together to form a strong, elastic skin on the water. This is called surface tension and it helps some animals actually walk on water. You've seen birds swim, but have you ever seen one walk across the top of the water? Coots have special feet with large lobes on their toes that help spread the birds' weight over the water's surface. Jacanas, crakes and gallinules walk across floating plants by spreading out their long toes. Some small lizards can run across the top of the water for a short distance before they sink down and swim. This helps them make a fast getaway if they are in danger.

Jacana

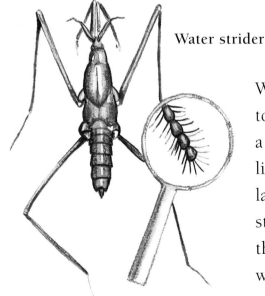

Water strider

Water striders, or pond skaters, seem to glide across the tops of ponds and marshes. If you look at their feet with a magnifying glass, you can see tufts of hairs that work like snowshoes, spreading the insects' weight over a larger area so they don't sink. Unlike most insects, water striders have claws partway up their legs instead of on their feet. Claws on their feet would break through the water's surface, making the water strider sink.

Will it float?

Here's an easy way to test the strength of the surface tension on water.

You should find that the needle sinks in the first glass because it is heavier than water and, when you dropped it in, you pierced the surface layer of water and broke the tension. In the second glass, the needle floats on the surface, supported by the strength of the surface tension. As long as the surface tension of the water is not broken, the needle — like the animals — will not sink.

1. Drop a needle into one glass of water and observe what happens.

2. In the second glass, carefully lay a needle lengthwise on top of the water. Be sure you don't poke the water's surface with the needle.

Hoppers and jumpers

If you had to jump everywhere instead of walk, you'd soon get tired. But if you were a flea, you could jump more than 10 000 times an hour and still have energy left over. Many animals use hopping and jumping to move quickly and escape enemies. In these pages you'll discover how their bodies are specially designed for making large leaps across the sand, over a plant or through an animal's fur. You'll also compare your jumping ability to that of this kangaroo rat and even smaller competitors, using a simple calculation. Your jump may look longer, but when it is compared to your height, who comes out the winner?

If you were a kangaroo rat ...

- you would have long, strong hind legs for jumping.
- you could jump up to 48 times your own body length in one leap.
- your long, tufted tail would help you balance and turn quickly in midair.
- you would have large, hairy hind feet to keep you from sinking in sand.
- you could travel up to 6 m (20 ft.) per second in a zigzag pattern to escape predators.

Springs and things

If you could jump as well as a grasshopper can, you would be able to travel the length of a football field in just three jumps. Insects such as grasshoppers, leafhoppers and fleas can leap a long way because they have strong leg muscles and small bodies that don't weigh very much. A flea's body is so thin that it can easily hop between an animal's hairs. A springtail has extra built-in equipment for jumping. Folded underneath its abdomen is a forked "tail" that flips down and pushes off the ground like a spring to shoot the insect through the air.

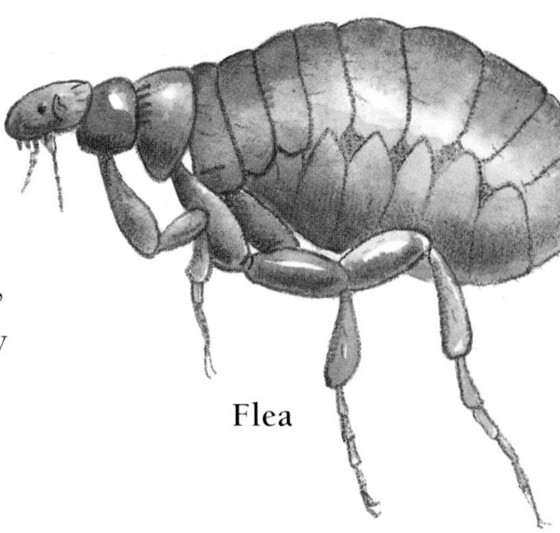

Flea

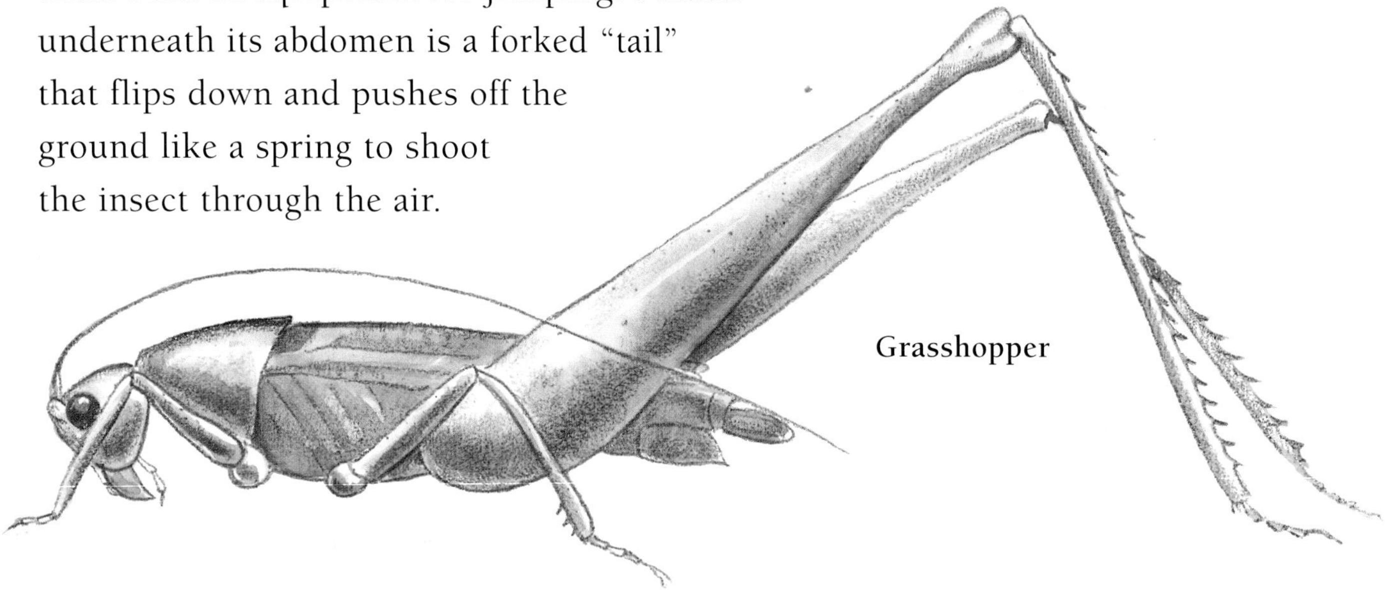

Grasshopper

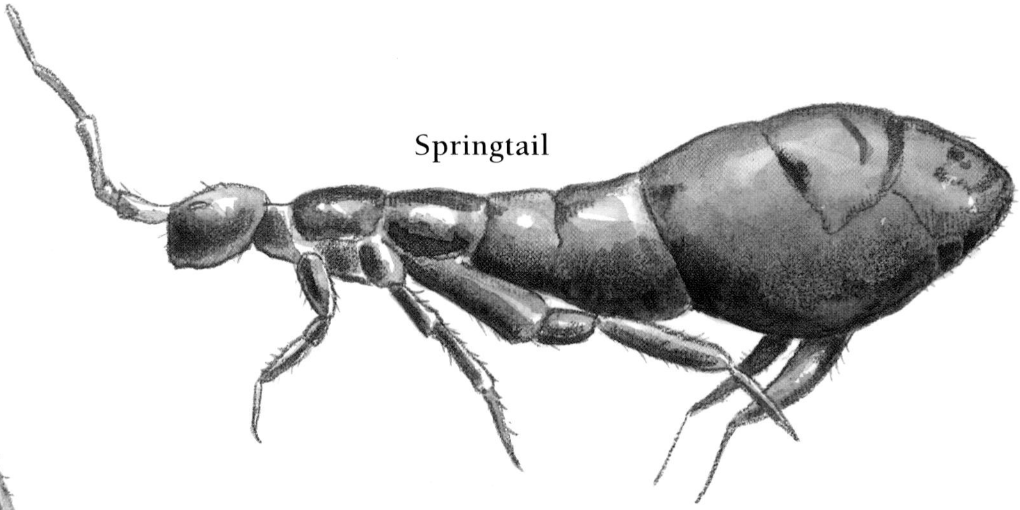

Springtail

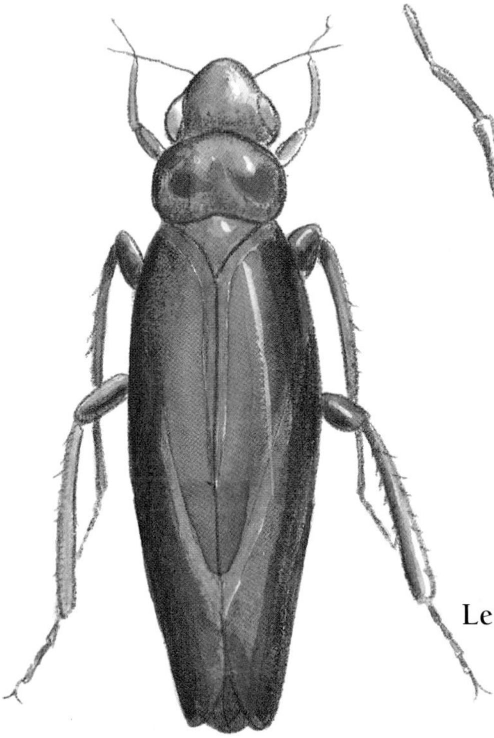

Leafhopper

Measuring up

Find out how you can measure your own jumps and compare them to these mini-Olympians.

You'll need:

a string about 1 m (3 ft.) long

a tape measure

tape

a calculator

1. In an open space, stretch a piece of string across the floor and tape each end down so that it stays in place.

2. Stand with your toes just touching the string and jump forward as far as you can, landing on your feet.

3. Have a friend measure the distance from the string to where your toes landed.

4. Measure your height without shoes on.

5. Figure out how far you can jump compared to your height by doing the following calculation. Where do you fit into the chart below?

Distance jumped (cm or in.) ÷ Height (cm or in.) = Number of body lengths jumped

Long distance leapers

Grasshopper	Flea	Leafhopper	Springtail
30	40	100	200

Number of body lengths traveled in one jump

Hop to it!

What's faster than a speeding bicycle and able to leap tall fences in a single bound? The answer is a kangaroo or a hare. Big, strong hind legs and large feet help kangaroos and hares jump high, leap long distances and travel quickly to escape predators. A Red Kangaroo can hop up to 48 km/h (30 m.p.h.) for short distances, while a Snowshoe Hare can briefly reach a speed of 80 km/h (50 m.p.h.) — as fast as a car on the highway. To make it even harder to catch them, hares and kangaroos hop in a zigzag pattern.

Kangaroo

High jumpers

Get a friend to help you measure how high you can jump from a standing start. Have your friend hold up a measuring stick or tape beside you. Jump as high as you can and have your friend mark the height of your feet on the stick. A kangaroo can jump 2.5 m (8 ft.) high from a standing start, and a Snowshoe Hare can reach 4.5 m (15 ft.). How do you compare?

Do you hop on one foot or two? If a kangaroo is not in a hurry, it uses all four feet and its tail to hop along. To speed up, a kangaroo lifts its front feet, holds its tail out behind for balance and jumps on its hind feet. If you check the tracks of a Snowshoe Hare in the snow, you'll see that its small front feet land one at a time behind its pair of large hind feet. When the hare jumps, its hind feet come forward past its front feet and land together. Its extra-large, hairy feet help keep the hare from sinking in the snow.

Snowshoe Hare

Snowshoe Hare tracks

Slippers and sliders

Kids ride down the slides in a playground just for fun, but some animals slide wherever they go. Snakes and other legless animals are experts at sliding their way across the ground and even up trees in search of food or to escape danger. Some creatures, such as earthworms, slugs and snails, prefer to come out in the rain because the wet ground is easier for them to move on. Read on to find out how this snail makes its own slippery trail during dry weather.

If you were a snail ...

- you would have only one muscular foot.
- your body would release a slimy mucus onto the ground to make a slippery trail for you to slide on. The trail would also help you find your way home.
- you would move very slowly, about 2.5 cm (1 in.) per minute.
- you would avoid rough and dry surfaces.

Slithering snakes

Lie face down on the floor with your arms pressed tightly against your sides. Try to slide across the floor like a snake, without using your feet or hands. Having trouble? That's because your body isn't adapted to move the way a snake does. If you run a finger down the middle of a friend's back, you'll feel the backbone, a ridge of 32 small bones called vertebrae. Snakes also have backbones, and large snakes may have up to 500 vertebrae. The more vertebrae in its backbone, the more flexible the snake is and the more easily it can move around. Snakes move in many different ways depending on where they live. For instance, desert snakes almost jump across hot sand, but garter snakes slide through wet grass. Check out the snake moves on these pages.

Boa Constrictor

The Smooth Green Snake anchors its tail on the ground with its belly scales and shoots its head and body forward. Once its neck is on the ground, the body folds up like an accordion, and the tail moves forward. This is known as concertina motion.

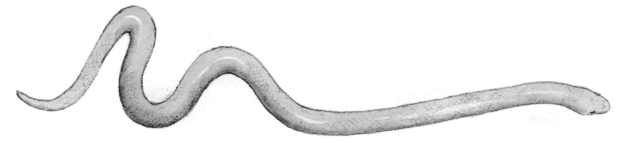

Smooth Green Snake

The Boa Constrictor slides ahead in a straight line, using caterpillar motion. The Constrictor stretches its body forward and grips the ground with some of its large belly scales. The rest of the body is then pulled along to "catch up."

The garter snake pushes against stones and other objects to move its body in an S-shape over the ground, in what is called serpentine movement.

Garter snake

Sidewinder

The Colorado Desert Sidewinder loops its body sideways across loose or hot sand, in a motion called sidewinding.

Cool moves

People use skis or skates to move quickly over snow or ice, but otters just need to use their large, webbed feet. Otters are at home in the water, but they are also very fast on land, especially in winter. To travel quickly across the ice and snow, they take three jumps and then slide up to 7 m (23 ft.). Otters can reach speeds of 28 km/h (17 m.p.h.) across a frozen lake.

Otter

Otter families often slide on their bellies down a frozen trail on the bank of a lake or river, with their front legs stretched out and their hind legs trailing. The otters take turns whooshing down the icy path again and again. In the summer, otters slide down mud trails and land in the water below.

Seal

The wide, webbed flippers of seals and walruses are ideal for swimming, but when these animals come on shore in the winter they have to slide across the ice to get around. Walruses use their large tusks like ice picks to pull themselves out of the water onto the ice. They can also turn their hind flippers forward on land to help them move around.

Walrus

Climbers and swingers

Kids aren't the only ones who like to climb trees. Many kinds of animals spend their lives eating, sleeping and moving through the treetops around the world. One tropical forest can be home to a huge variety of creatures, some living right at the tops of the trees, others midway, and some near the ground. Animals that spend their days feeding on the ground may take to the trees at night to sleep, where they are safer from predators. Some animals' bodies are specially suited for swinging through trees or holding on to the branches.

If you were a tree frog ...

- you would have long, slim hind legs for climbing, walking and leaping.
- your toes would end in sticky round pads, like suction cups, to help you hang on as you climb.
- your toes could swivel sideways and backward so you could climb without having to let go.
- you could change color to blend in with your surroundings. This would help you hide from predators and sneak up on prey.

Tree trapeze

Swinging across the monkey bars in the playground would be a lot easier if you were built like a Spider Monkey. Their extra-long arms and long, flexible fingers and toes are perfect for reaching out and grabbing branches as they swing through the trees. Spider Monkeys and gibbons have special hands that are bent into a hook shape to make it easier to grasp the next branch. A gibbon can travel very quickly through the trees and can cover more than 6 m (20 ft.) during one swing.

Gibbon

Several tree climbers have very talented tails. Spider Monkeys use their long tails like an extra arm for holding on. Their tails have a rough, hairless tip that helps them grasp branches as they travel from tree to tree. Opossums and pangolins also use their tails for support when climbing and hanging from a tree branch.

Spider Monkey

Slow down

The Three-toed Sloth is the slowest mammal on Earth. It hangs upside down from tree branches, holding on with huge, curved claws, and moves only about 1.8 m (6 ft.) per minute. To find out how slow a sloth really is, measure off a distance of 1.8 m (6 ft.) and have a friend time how long it takes you to walk it at your normal speed. Now slow down and take a full minute to cover the same distance. Try the same thing while moving upside down along some monkey bars or a tree branch. Now that's slow!

Three-toed Sloth

Index